Just Two Years

Reflections of Young Motherhood

C. M. Palmer

Made with ❤ on the BookLeaf Publishing Platform
www.bookleafpub.in
www.bookleafpub.com

Dedication

To my mother, Jessica, and to Julie.

And to my sisters.
I am overjoyed and honored to embrace motherhood
alongside you.

Preface

When I told my husband I wanted to participate in a writing challenge, and complete a book of poetry with a deadline in twenty-one days, he looked at me at said, "If it's not perfect, can you be ok with that?" He knows me well, what can I say. I told him yes, because I decided that my attitude going into this would be one of seeing the beauty in this season of young motherhood. I purposed to see beauty in what I could come up with in my spare moments, and see whatever imperfections made it past some limited editing as an accurate representation of the busyness of life. I have been refreshed creatively and mentally by this exercise. It has given me intentional space to reflect on life and be grateful. It is truly a beautiful thing!

Acknowledgements

Ty, thank you for always supporting me in my creative
endeavors.
I would not have done this without your encouragement.

Lydia, thank you for your input on this, and for listening
to me ramble.

The Wonder of My Son

His eyes are full of wonder,
His eagerness contagious.
He often stops to ponder
Those new things he finds outrageous.

He sees each day as an adventure waiting.
"I had a good sleep," he'll say.
Stumbling out of bed lacking all clothing,
He's already prepared to take on the day.

He just wants to contribute,
To conversation, to work, and to play.
His intensity is a favorite attribute,
He simply wants to have a say.

He is a bottomless well of stories,
He's a master of concoction.
None of his characters are phonies,
But they do come with an interchanging option.

The yarns he spins never lack in ardor.
He's not restrained by self-consciousness.
His bountiful expressions are refreshing in their candor.
He's learning to temper himself with gentleness.

He gives life's details tremendous thought.
He has big feelings. Big emotions. A big heart.
Expressing it all can be a lot
But his efforts to do so set him apart.

There's no false motive in his smile.
His heart is warm and unaffected.
His consideration holds no guile.
His tenderness on us all projected.

He's as articulate as a toddler can be.
His vocabulary is extensive.
His desire to learn astounds me.
I try never to be dismissive.

I have a responsibility
To foster his interests, his queries.
To feed that spark of curiosity
No matter how outlandish his theories.

His imagination is a gift to many,
It blesses us with joy.
His intuition is uncanny.
I treasure the heart of my little boy.

Struggles of Today

I rarely have the words
To voice the struggles of each day.
My vocabulary unequipped
With the how and what to say.
I know that I felt smothered,
By the constant ask for play,
But I also felt the love and joy
That in his eyes I could assay,
When my little son of two
On my shoulder paused to lay.
There are always duties waiting,
On my mind they always weigh.
He does not see my conflict
As I try desperately to persuade
Him that I have other things to do
And cannot always stop to play.
I see his disappointment
And assure to him and say
That I can banter just as soon
As these tasks are finished for the day.
When I do take the time to listen
When my son wants to parlay,
He awakes in me a smile
That I cannot chase away.

Somehow giving him a space to speak
Often keeps my own despair at bay.
I know that I felt claustrophobic
With the baby strapped to me all day,
But I've never seen such unaffected
Adoration directed my way.
She looks at me with total trust,
At my feet her little heart does lay.
The deep honor of nurturing her
Nothing can at all outweigh.
I know that when I see myself
I see a woman oft in disarray,
Who hasn't had time to shower
And who's under eyes are grey.
I fight off a little twinge,
A deep catch within my airway.
There is a part of me that misses
That girl with no spit up on display,
But when I think again
that narrative begins to fray.
That girl was not bothered
With things outside of her own soirée
Of worries, cares, and come-aparts,
From these she could not break away.
Her anxious self would have gawked
At what I now accomplish in a day.
She wasn't lazy or ungrateful,

But she could not see the interplay
Of responsibility and and joy.
Her fulfilment was a fickle colorway
That faded like a rainbow when clouded just a touch.
She didn't know what I know today.
I've lived more than her and experienced
Much more than I can convey in this little wordplay.
I wouldn't go back, not for a minute.
Please give me my unwashed flyaways.
This depth of fulfilment and bottomless grace
Does not break down, diminish, decay.
It grows and grows and grows still more,
Every single, blessed day.
As I grow, they grow, we grow, side by side.
Each day is a holy day,
With a holy calling and holy empowerment,
On His strength I must my weary self lay.
I've still much to learn, He asks me to trust
In Him the Potter, as soft clay.
He's given me a husband, children, these duties.
He will guide me through each byway.
He will never forsake me, never neglect me.
He alone is my Mainstay.
So maybe I need to worry less,
About voicing my struggles each day.
Maybe I should kiss my man the second he gets home.
He'll laugh when I recount the parlay and the play.

I'll listen while he talks of work,
We can chatter and assuage
Our tiredness and fears together,
Take time to sing and pray.
I will rest my arms and back,
When with her papa she can stay.
She's only this small once,
I should look down and not wish away
This little girl at my breast,
Instead caress her head and say,
That I will be right here when she needs me.
I will give my son an attentive ear and a space to say
All those matters on his growing mind.
I will let him on my shoulder lay.
Maybe I need to rejoice in the work
That I have to do each day.
Voice to my Savior the overwhelm and
Cling with stubborn faith to my Mainstay.
There will always be enough grace to cover
The struggles of today.

Somehow

"She is just a little baby, somehow."
I'm not sure if it was the keen perception or
perhaps the grownup choice of words, that made me
stop and smile.
It had been my two-year old's observation that caused
me to reflect.
He said it just like that, "She is just a little baby,
somehow."
The setting was more than a little comical,
He was perched on the porcelain throne attending to
business of some importance.
I wish now that I could remember why he said it, but I
don't.
What he said was astute enough that I wrote it down to
come back to.
Maybe it seemed so specifically truthful and compelling
because I've thought that myself, "She is just a little
baby, somehow."
She is.
Little in a delightful, chunky way.
And she's certainly a baby.
Complete with rosy cheeks that are so blubberifically
delightful that they pull her full lips down and open at
all times.

"She is just a little baby, somehow."

Somehow.

Somehow this little girl, animated by the breath of life, is half me, half her papa.

Somehow her big brother sitting on the toilet all by his big boy self is too.

Somehow, I'm their mother.

Somehow, they are my own two children.

Somehow, I'm living in a dream just that perfect.

One Just Once

You only have one once,
That time is metamorphosizing.
You enter it just newly crowned,
With motherly matrondom demanding.

You only have one once,
It's a bittersweet reflection.
Those days spent just the two of us
Were filled with sweet, complete connection.

You only have one once,
It's a time unlike the rest,
Somehow just as full and busy
As now when with two I'm blessed.

You only have one once,
I've seen God's grace in this,
I needed this time to mature,
To not acknowledge this would be remiss.

You only have one once,
It's a season that for most will pass.
It will end and change into another,
New and different joys my task.

You only have one once,
Little One we don't have much time,
Another one is joining us
In this next fall time.

You only have one once,
For me that time has passed,
That foundation of relationship
I pray we've built to last.

You only have one once,
I treasure the gift of those years,
And the experience it gave me,
All the laughs and all the tears.

You only have one once,
Lord, thank You for that time.
Those early years of motherhood,
Those fires that refine.

You only have one once,
My metamorphosis has just begun.
Forever and into eternity
Will I cherish those two years with one.

Matters of To Do

It'll take just a second.
"Wait a minute," I tell you.
Just let me clean up,
There's still more to do.

Whoops I forgot
That pile of mail.
I still need to dump
That dirty mop pail.

One task to the next.
There's always something to do.
I forget how many times
I've said "Just wait" to you.

Sometimes you scream
To remind me you're there.
There's just so much to do
I have no time to care.

I shrug you off.
You change up your tactics.
Now I'm mad because my busy
Is disrupted by your antics.

We quarrel. You cry.
There's still much to do.
I ask myself, Why?
Am I so flustered by you?

I take a few breaths.
I remember what matters.
It's not the mop or the mail,
Not while you are in tatters.

I should've stopped all
The first time you asked.
My attention is yours now.
Little One, with you I am tasked.

I wrap you up in a hug.
I whisper, "I'm here.
I wasn't before and I'm sorry.
I should've stayed near."

The dishes can wait.
There's still much to do.
But what truly matters--
My child, is you.

Canvas of Adventure

My baby is a human canvas and
By the end of every day,
There are splotches of a story
That tells of all his play.

I spy a bit of egg yolk
Pasted on his rosy chub.
It tells of yummy tastings
And no shortage of good grub.

A splash of crusty brown
Upon his little arm,
I see a muddy exploration
Lured by puddle's charm.

His hair is tossed and tussled,
A regular bird's nest.
It is a condensed collection
Of things gathered on his quest.

A piece of hay. A twist of twine.
There's a spotted feather.
And sprinkled generously throughout
There's grit blown in by weather.

Into the tub he goes,
His canvas is wiped clean,
Yet inside his little mind,
Remain good memories unseen.

I Made My Mother Cry Once

I made my mother cry once.
I had some help of course.
Two brothers and a sister,
My trustiest cohorts.

Let me set the scene here,
Of that fateful winter day,
That would go down in history as
Truly epic, so they say.

A fresh blanket of snow,
Had fallen just that night.
An empty irrigation pond
Was what we held in sight.

It's sloping sides were perfect,
For a sledding day of fun.
So we bundled up and went outside,
Hauling sleds while on the run.

We started in the morning,
It was truly bitter cold,
But by the afternoon there was

No snow left to behold.

The winter sun had warmed,
Our playground quickly melted.
What we now were sledding in
Was a muddy, mushy wetland.

Complete with thick jungle,
Of cattails and pheasants.
We stormed through the brush,
Flushing the birds with no hesitance.

Our snow pants and coats
Were well plastered with muck.
But you couldn't hardly tell now!
What wonderful luck!

For instead of brown slush,
Engulfing ourselves,
We now were quite plush,
In a fluffy coating of cattails.

We packed up our gear,
Satisfied with our conquest.
The petrified pheasants
Returned to their nests.

We were blissfully unaware
That'd we'd been tarred and then feathered.
Our warm winter clothes were
Unequipped for this sort of weather.

We gave no thought to our appearance,
As we trudged back to the door.
Our thoughts were only of supper, but
Our mother's face struck fear to each core.

She opened the screen,
Froze there on the step.
An expression of horror,
Across her features swept.

She did not say a word,
That I can remember.
She just gathered the mess,
And gave us time to consider.

We realized our error,
Hung our heads in remorse.
We should've known better.
We regretted our course.

We were as quiet as mice.
As meek as Moses of old.

As our mother undressed us,
We did exactly as told.

I made my mother cry once,
As she knelt over the tub.
Hot tears mixed with fluffy mud,
As our clothes she did scrub.

Envy

Envy is a little thing
That creeps in on the sly.
It'll sometimes take me ages
To see it standing by.

It whispers in my ear.
It digs and pries and pokes,
At all those lies that I keep near,
Those untruths that I have spoke.

It prods my insecurities.
Exploits then justifies my fears.
It sows deep discontentment,
As angst inside me leers.

It will twist a loving offer
Into a plotting guise.
A kind word into a signifier
Of some sinister enterprise.

It skillfully contorts the faces
Of trustworthy friends around
Into a blur of suspicions.
Good intent it will confound.

Give it an inch it will take a mile,
Each and every time.
Its pettiness is juvenile.
Its true face it can't disguise.

Take every thought captive
That is the offense
The defense the only way to
Combat the nonsense.

Those lies, do not repeat.
Do not give them space to grow.
My own destruction will be replete
If I do not uproot this dire foe.

With truth replace each lie.
Fill soul and heart and mind,
With the assurances of God's own Word.
In Him eternal peace I find.

Only He can vanquish my envy,
That dark shadow of reflection.
Only He can wage and levy
Total annihilation against that abstraction.

I need not covet another's life,

Position, or gifts, or face.
I am fashioned uniquely in His image,
He does not His artistry misplace.

Messes and Mayhem and Glory

Let me tell a story,
Of mayhem and messes and glory.
These three things ever the mission
Of a small boy's ambition.
No, he will not deviate,
To alter at all might alleviate
The guts and the glory
Without these where's the story?
Onward and upward.
Toward danger forward.
Upon his valor he will lean
As he marches on to vict'ries unseen.
I observe him outside,
(Over his safety I preside,)
A silent cheerleader,
My allegiance does not waver,
His courage has captured my heart,
As well as his spirit, quite tart.
I look on in amusement,
Watching his movement,
He's just now diverting his course
'Cause what could be worse
Then missing that puddle

No indeed that would muddle
His plan for the day
That he just this second did lay.
Surely a boy must have a say
In the how and the what of his play?
For its mayhem and messes and glory
That will make the most glorious story,
A story I can't wait to hear
As it grows bigger and older each year.
There is no greater joy
Than to watch my little boy
Grow into a man without fear
Keeping honor and valor near.
So I will encourage
His honor and courage,
And train him up in the way he should go,
Cheer him on as he battles each foe.
Go 'cross the puddle,
Don't let adversity muddle
That clear calling upon your life.
Always seek peace and not strife,
But never cower in fear,
In His power your victory will always be near.

Time In a Day

I'm sure we've all heard someone say,
"There's not enough time in a day."
Let's be honest, you've said it, I've said it too,
"There's not enough time, there's too much to do."
Well I'm here to challenge that adage,
Because I think, no, I know it does damage.
Our minds will repeat only what we allow,
Those words are not worth the sweat off our brow.
Each day we wake up is a gift from above,
And I am certain that God in His infinite love,
Did not short us one second, one minute, one hour,
Not in His great mercy, not in His all-knowing power.
He set the stars in the sky with one word from his
mouth,
He fashioned four corners: North, East, West and South.
He set the earth on its axis, He made it to spin.
How arrogant are we to think He just won't let us win?
How many fewer our worries, how joyous each day,
If we chose to believe and decided to say,
That there is always just enough time in a day.

Just Two Years

Just two years ago I became a new mother.
My whole self reborn at his birth.
My purpose, perspective, place, Oh the Wonder
Inspired by him and the advent of childbirth.

The Wonder never ceases but reaches ever deeper
Into the unseen, before unknown, recesses of my soul.
He's taught me, stretched me, loved me, unlike any other,
His demands broke me apart and made me a new whole.

We forged a relationship, teacher and teacher,
New graces empowered this bond.
I felt overcome by this calling much higher,
Compelled by an all-consuming passion to respond.

It's been two whole years of laughter
From a pure spring of delight
As a family, Child, Mother and Father
Each discovering more of their own birthright.

It was one year ago, as we looked toward the future,
We saw another soul had been charged to our care.
We waited to know if it was a he or a her,
A joyful anticipation, two dreams to compare.

As did my waistline so did my heart grow larger,
Perhaps more with anxieties than affections.
Peace and contentment I worked to foster
Amid a toddler and life and distractions.

As the advent drew nearer, our new reality became
clearer,
Our family was taking new shape.
Our trajectory forward but not linear,
All sides were expanding into an unfamiliar landscape.

And yet all the edges, every expanse, every corner,
Shone with the ready, unreadiness of love.
That steady, unsteady, glorious shimmer
That illuminates the dark unknown we're afraid of.

Finally that night came and fell as my pains grew closer
That new, little soul on its way.
My husband held me and I held on to his whisper
"Baby's almost here...Baby's on its way."

The intensity of that singular sensation is unlike any
other
Time is lost, the concept forgotten,
There is simply wave upon wave I must master
With the end in sight, the reward nearly gotten.

Soon that singular sensation was buried under
A complexity of feelings so sweet
Through all the pains came not a single thing bitter
The utter completeness of that moment replete.

My son had been asleep but stumbled out of his bedcover
Just in time to witness this advent of miraculous end.
He was there as I cried and introduced his new sister,
There is no moment of history that could with this
moment contend.

Just three months ago I lay with my daughter
Just minutes old, at peaceful rest on my breast.
My husband, my son, and my own mother,
Surrounded me, spoke love and life, held and caressed.

In these past three months there has been twice as much
laughter
As we have ever heard or taken part in before.
Little Miss and Little Man look a lot like each other,
But of other similarities you'll find no more.

It's been two whole years since I became a mother,
Two years of life done right and done wrong.
As I look into their eyes I can do naught else but wonder
At the beauty and the life and it makes my heart long.

Long for each day that together we'll wander,
Living and doing and expanding
Our purpose, our place, our perspective, our wonder.
At the fullness, the beauty, the joys never ending.

I long for the strength to never falter
To never fail them or hurt them at all.
I've seen my imperfectness, that I can't alter,
But I will show them His grace when I fall.

I long for two more years, I pray to the Father,
For time with these babes that He's given.
I keep a space for one child I haven't yet met,
And keep faith that they are safely in Heaven.

It took just two years a whole New World to enter
To be filled with this fullness astounding.
I pray that the song of my heart never falter.
That it ever shout out with worship resounding.

Matron of Memories

She's the Matron of Memories,
She guards them with care.
She arranges life's harmonies
You may not notice are there.

She keeps out the weeds,
Tirelessly, vigilantly she pulls.
She plants instead good seeds.
Her gardens are small souls.

She gives of herself,
To fill up their day
With good food and good health,
Warm caresses and play.

She's careful to shower
More praise than reproof.
When she listens she kneels lower
So as not to be aloof.

She is a creator of fun,
An instigator of creativity.
Her task never done,
Memory making requires longevity.

As those small souls grow older,
Their needs grow as well.
With love, wisdom, and laughter,
Their dependency she works to dispel.

Their hearts and their minds
She both guards and expands.
They're retaining more and more of their finds,
And she helps them to sift through the sands.

She's the Matron of Memories,
She will not leave her post,
Her mind retains those past notabilities.
Of her marvelous children she'll forever boast.

She is a library of generations,
Past and Present she does tend,
She is a Mother of Nations,
Her faithfulness reaches into Future's end.

She is the Matron of Memories,
We see her throughout all time.
She is but a mother of committed strength,
Rightfully enshrined in history's song and rhyme.

Burdens Light

God, let my vanity be shorn
From my weary, sinful self.
In Your own flesh You have borne
Away my pride again.
I die to self each day.
Your burden let me carry,
For it is light, straight is the way.
Of what I must be wary
Your Word illuminates to me.
It's bright truth dispelling darkness.
At Your feet I bend my knee
To praise You for Your faithfulness.
It is unwavering in its nature,
Your own nature compels it to
Continue on and nurture,
'Til your children's hearts are made new.
You are the First and Last,
The Author of all time.
Abiding in the future and the past
Ever present in eternal glories sublime.

To My Mother

Your face grows ever lovelier,
With the passing of the years.
You are a speaker of truth and hope,
To your children and your peers.

Your selflessness inspires me
To press on every day.
You have chosen us over yourself,
You have taken the more honorable way.

I've seen you rocked by grief
I could not comprehend.
Yet still you found tenderness within yourself
As to us all I watched you tend.

Your eyes shine bright with life,
Your heart is bold with passion.
I'm grateful for God's artful hand
When my mother He did fashion.

I've looked to you for guidance,
You've faithfully steered me straight.
You raised me up to know the Lord,
To enter in at that little gate.

Your children arise up,
Your husband at your side,
Together we will testify of those virtues
Which within your heart reside.

You've been my rock unmoving,
Through storms and stillness equal,
You're witness to my journey,
The prequel, present, and the sequel.

In a single faithfulness of purpose,
You nurtured me as a child small,
And still you shape me with your wisdom,
You keep me steady when I fall.

I've felt your disapproval,
But never your disgust.
You've loved like Christ,
Your forgiveness constant and robust.

You held my hand in childbirth,
You've cried when I felt loss.
In strength you've ever pointed me
Back to His holy cross.

You've led by your example,

Your submission to the Lord.
I am here now to witness
That great is your reward.

Touches of Faithfulness

You raised a fine young man.
He is strong and kind, I will attest.
As his wife and friend,
I am exceptionally blessed.

I see how your words checked him,
Guided him in his youth.
I am grateful that you taught him
To always walk in truth.

Your faithfulness as a mother
Touches more than just your son.
My children have a wonderful father:
Committed, loving, wise, and fun.

Your example of hard work
Taught him to persevere.
I've seen him stick it out in hardship,
He does what's right without fear.

I have a husband who is generous,
He is loving, good and true.
I think his mother more than deserves,

A hearty "Well done" and a "Thank You."

To the Man Who Made Me a Mother

To the man who made me a mother,
You've realized all my dreams.
Together we have stitched a life
Bursting full with love at all its seams.

To the man who made me a mother,
Your eyes still find mine and speak
A depth of understanding that I pray
Will grow forever but never peak.

To the man who made me a mother,
My dear lover and companion,
As I watch you blossom as a father
My very soul you champion.

To the man who made me a mother,
May our closeness ever grow,
Into an unquenchable fire of devotion
Stronger than what we've ever known.

To the man who made me a mother,
The second half of my heart.
To you I have committed myself

Until death do us part.

To the man who made me a mother,
Who chose me for this grand partnership,
I vow to choose you every day,
To never undermine our friendship.

To the man who made me a mother,
May we raise our children well,
May our example lead them steady on
In war and peace, in still and swell.

To the man who made me a mother,
Can you believe these two new faces?
Would you have ever thought we'd make it?
Be more in love? Have found our places?

To the man who made me a mother,
Together we stand a living witness,
Of the faithfulness of a good God who
Has orchestrated this life by His loving-kindness.

To the man who made me a mother,
May we age with grace and wisdom.
United in all that is right and good.
Looking forward towards that Kingdom.

To the man who made me a mother,
May our eyes never lose their speaking.
May our children never question our loyalty.
To know each other better may we die still seeking.

To See the Beauty In a Thing

To see the beauty in a thing,
Be it old, new, dirty, clean,
Is a thing of beauty in itself.
Surely a nobler way of being.
I don't mean delusion or dishonesty,
Or living in a land of make-believe,
But of seeing it all, the good and the bad,
And dwelling on the good.
In a fallen place to remain transfixed
By the Creator and His glory.

Legacy

I have had the distinct privilege,
Of knowing many women in my lineage.
They have left to me a heritage,
Of strength and beauty and grace.

Daughters, sisters, mothers all,
To fill theirs shoes I must stand tall.
I will pass on their histories and enthrall
My children with their courage.

I do not take it lightly,
These women and their insight godly,
Their gift of wisdom ever timely,
As I walk within their footsteps.

Their character speaks for itself,
They endowed their children with great wealth
Of kindness, resilience and integrity of inner self.
May I too, pass on these gifts.

I am proud that their likenesses I bear,
Their strong features are reflected there
In the mirror where I stand and stare,
Reminded of their legacies.

It is a thing of beauty to reflect
On the dots that all connect
Me to them, I won't neglect
The examples they have left me.

I will learn from their mistakes,
From their triumphs and I'll take
Great care to mend and break
As I leave a heritage myself.

Their memory will not fade away,
It will be enshrined and stay
In those stories which do portray
The legacy they've left.